Contents

Introduction

arming isn't what it used to be.

A hundred years ago, horses pulled the plow as the farmer walked behind, guiding the blade through acres of soil. Men wore thick gloves to tear ears of corn from crunchy stalks, then women shucked those ears with bare hands. Early risers went to the hen house every day to gather eggs in a basket. Cows let down milk squirt by squirt, into individual pails, while the milkers who kneaded the animals' teats squatted on stools beside their warm flanks.

Technological advancements, especially in farm equipment, have made these tasks and almost all other farm work much less labor intensive. Bigger, better, faster machines mean it takes fewer people and less time to do just about every job. That certainly doesn't mean today's farmers work less than their predecessors.

On the contrary, it means farmers are now able to plow that many more acres, pick and shuck that many more ears of corn, gather that many more eggs, milk that many more cows.

As farmers' efficiency has increased, so has the size and scale of the average farm operation. The myriad 100-acre farms of a hundred years ago have given way to a smaller number of 500-plus-acre farms of the twenty-first century. And these bigger farms are owned and worked by fewer people. United States Department of Agriculture statistics tell us that farmers made up 31 percent of the U.S. labor force in 1910, and the average farm size was 138 acres. Forty years later, only about 12 percent of the U.S. labor force was involved in farming, and the average farm size was 216 acres. In the 1990s, only about 3 percent of the U.S. labor force were farmers, and the average farm was about 460 acres.

Advances in technology have also brought farmers to an age of specialization. In the early twentieth century, the typical farmer raised a variety of crops and livestock. If the market price of corn or wheat fell, there was always the money milk brought in. Hogs were raised alongside dairy cows, sheep alongside beef cattle.

Hand milking

In the days when each cow was milked by hand, dairy herds were much smaller than on today's farms.

Because farming was done on a smaller scale, selling a couple bales of wool or a few dozen eggs was worth a farmer's while.

Despite these changes, however, much of farming is exactly how it used to be. The moo of the cow is still low and musical, and a piglet's surprised squeal is still high and piercing. The rows of tilled soil are as rich and black when seen from atop a John Deere Model D as from atop a John Deere 9000T. Corn shoots still poke up through the earth tender and green, a couple of weeks after the seeds are planted. Alfalfa and clover grow as thick and abundant as they ever did, and they smell just as fresh and grassy when they are mowed. Springtime will always be green, autumn harvests will always be golden. The deep sense of satisfaction that comes from putting in a day—or a season—of honest hard work, from reaping what has been sown, remains the same. The belief that farming is an honorable, worthwhile way of life is timeless.

Pictures from the Farm is about all these aspects of farming life—both those that have changed and those that remain the same.

On one hand, the pictures in this book offer a wistful, nostal-

Shearing machine
A hand crank powered the razors of sheep farms in the early 1900s.

gic look at what life was like when Mom's stove was cast iron, when the Thanksgiving turkey came from the farm's own flock, and when corn relish was canned in jars. The images recall the days of community threshing crews, tractors with hand cranks and steel wheels, spring houses and ice houses, and stoves heated with wood and corn cobs. Anyone who has lived on a farm in the early part of the twentieth century will recognize their lives in these pages.

On the other hand, the images tell a timeless tale of tractor nuts and bolts, new-mown hay, blue skies, muddy roads, daily chores, striped overalls and rolled up sleeves, red barns and sprawling farmstead—all of which are still hallmarks of today's farms.

Some of the images in this book have specific dates attached to them, and these pictures testify as to what people, places, and activities were like at the time the photograph was taken. Other pictures need no specific date; these photographs show details of farming life that were as true in the early to mid-1900s as they are today. When and where these photographs were taken is much less important than what they show.

None of the photographs in this volume are historical recreations. All of the equipment, activities, buildings, and other details belong to the time when the photograph was taken. Most of the photographs were taken between 1900 and the 1950s.

Like a family album, *Pictures from the Farm* collects many individual moments—memories of the people, places, and activities—between two covers to create a single, honest portrait of the farming life and pay tribute to those who lived it.

About J. C. Allen & Son

For nearly 100 years, the photographers of J. C. Allen & Son have captured the indelible impressions of farm life—from the glorious fields to the mundane privy behind the farmhouse. No aspect of the farm and those who lived there has escaped their artistic eyes and sharp camera lenses.

In 1904, J. C. Allen bought a Kodak camera to take pictures on his trip to the World's Fair in St. Louis, Missouri. Soon after, he got a large wooden view camera that sat on a wooden tripod and made pictures on 5 x 7-inch glass plates. Next he got a hand-held Press Graflex camera. These same cameras were used by J. C. Allen for a half a century, capturing countless images of rural life.

J. C. Allen was originally employed by Purdue University for his knowledge of livestock judging. He used his cameras to take pictures of livestock. When an editor of a farm publication in one of the southern states asked if he could buy one of his pictures to use in the magazine, Allen's photography business was born.

In 1929, Chester P. Allen graduated from Purdue University and joined his father in the picture business, becoming the "Son" in J. C. Allen & Son. He spent his entire life taking pictures of farm-related subjects, just as his father had done.

Chester's son, John O. Allen, worked part time in the family business while in college and, after graduating from Purdue's school of agriculture, began to work full time. In 1970, the business was officially incorporated as J. C. Allen & Son, Inc.

Three generations
The three J. C. Allen & Son, Inc. photographers spent most of their time behind their cameras, but in 1970, all three stepped in front of the camera lens for a three-generation portrait. From left to right, John O. Allen, John C. Allen, and Chester P. Allen.

But the Allens didn't just view farming life through the camera lens. Descended from a long line of farmers, all the photographers were involved in agriculture throughout their lives. They owned farmland in the heart of the Midwest, closely following and participating in the grain and livestock markets. Today, John O. Allen lives in the country, where he has tractors and several horses that he rides regularly, like the folks the Allens had captured on film.

Over the years, the three photographers have traveled to all fifty states taking pictures. In the 1930s, they were among the first photographers to take pictures in color, but, until the 1960s, the vast majority of their images were captured as black-and-white prints.

Today, the J. C. Allen & Son archives cover the entire twentieth century and more than 77,000 subjects, including thousands showing the spirit of the farms' people, land, crops, animals, and machinery. The Allens's photos have been published in most major agricultural publications in the Midwest, as well as in many books, such as *This Old Farm, A Farm Country Christmas, 100 Years of Vintage Farm Tractors,* and *The Complete Pig* (all published by Voyageur Press).

It is with great pride and pleasure that J. C. Allen & Son shares its pictures with the readers of this book.

Best Wishes

John C. Allen

CHAPTER I

The Majesty of the Farmstead

Left:

Classic farmstead

A classic farmstead—a white, round-roof barn; tall gray silos; white fences; rolling cropland; and a pasture full of Guernseys—all under blue skies.

Above:

Taking shape

Workers frame up a gambrel roof for a large barn in 1933.

The Farmstead

Owning a Piece of the Earth

Left:

The original home-office

For the past hundred years, farming has been the quintessential way of achieving the popular dream of self-employment.

For a farmer, the daily commute is the walk between the farmhouse and the barn and the drive in the fields on a horse or tractor. "Office equipment" includes hay wagons, plows, separators, or combines; co-workers are family and neighbors. The land serves as both office space and business partner.

Below:

Details, details

A farm's prosperity can be measured in its details. Farming is a business venture, and most farmers first direct extra money back into their business, buying new equipment, livestock, or land, or expanding the barn and other working outbuildings. Only after they recover their initial investment do farmers have disposable income to spend on luxuries like fenced-in yards; wide, pillared porches; and carved house trim.

21

Acres of Glory

The Fields, the Crops, the Sky

Facing page:

Room to grow

Wide-open spaces attracted the first settlers to America's farm country. America was a land of plenty—with plenty of land. The plethora of space offered room for both crops and farmsteads to grow.

From the days of the first farmers to the early 1900s, when this picture was taken, to the present day, the fields have been a place where a person can feel firsthand the immensity and richness of the land. Here, the barley mower offers a front-row seat.

Right, top:

Row by row

A hay baler methodically combs up row after row of hay in the summer of 1947.

Right, bottom:

Patchwork

Contour farming—running crop rows across the slope of rolling hills—controls soil erosion, while turning the landscape into a green and gold patchwork.

The center of attention

Ask folks what the difference is between a homestead and a farmstead, and nearly everyone will say "the barn." This is not surprising, since all farm work eventually comes back to the barn.

No matter what their shape or size, all barns have a common primary function—storage. Whether horses, wagons, plows, tractors, loose hay, cloth bags full of grain, or heads of sheep and cattle, the barn houses both the implements and products of the farmer's livelihood. Given the essential role the barn plays in the farm family's business, many farmers give their barns as much money, time, and attention as their farmhouses—and sometimes more.

Below:

Dutch doors

This 1920s L-shaped livestock barn features Dutch doors: doors cut in half horizontally so that the top half can be opened to allow light and air to enter, but the bottom half can remain closed to keep cows in or out.

The Foundation of the Farmstead

The Barn and Its Features

Left:

Hay hoods

The ridge of this roof extends out to form a hay hood, from which the farmer hangs a pulley to lift bundles of loose hay into the hayloft. The overhang also provides protection for the hayloft doors.

Below:

Fresh air

With hundreds of cows shuffling about, the temperature inside a dairy barn can become unbearably hot and stifling, not to mention odorous, in the summer. Metal cupola ridge ventilators, like the ones lined up on the top ridges of these dairy barns, keep the air circulating out through the tops of barns.

Big Barns

Giants of the Landscape

Facing page:

A sign of good times

Unusually large barns, such as this one, require a large investment. Of course, the more prosperous the farm, the more crops that have to be stored and the more livestock (and feed) that has to be housed.

Left, top:

Living room

Living animals take up more space than harvested grains, so livestock barns are necessarily bigger than crop barns. Livestock farmers need not only room to house all their animals, but also room to store the grain and hay to feed all these animals.

Mr. Rupel's big barn holds 240 head of sheep.

Left, center:

Making an entrance

When housing both horses and sheep, as this barn did, it is best to have a couple sets of double doors. The advantage of this barn's sliding doors is that they can't be flung open by high winds as easily as hinged doors.

Left, bottom:

Adding on

Towering silos attached to two-story barns with arched gothic and gambrel roofs—this is what usually comes to mind when one pictures the barns of North America's midwestern dairy land.

The two-story, gambrel-roofed barn on the right is most likely this Illinois dairy barn's original structure, with the perpendicular wing added later as the herd increased in number. Building additions onto existing barns is an efficient, economical way to expand the space without having to build an entirely new barn.

When Form Weds Function

Strikingly Beautiful Barns

Right, top:

Common barn, uncommon flair

Although the barn is a utilitarian building, that doesn't stop farmers from exercising their creativity when building their barns. The gable roof is quite common, but the jaunty cupola ridge ventilator, windows with gable dormers, and diamond-shaped windows on the side doors give this barn a distinctive flair. Lightning rods, placed at either end of the roof ridge, were all the rage in the 1920s.

Right, bottom:

A farmer's barn is his castle

The castlelike turrets and archways of this stone dairy barn add grandeur to a 1920s Michigan farmstead.

Although brick and stone are often used for foundations, entire barns of stone and brick are less common than those of wood. Molding and baking bricks require more work than cutting down trees and sawing boards, as does digging up and moving stones. Bricks and stones are also heavier than wood, so more muscle is needed to haul and set them into place. Finally, the irregular shapes and sizes of individual stones make putting together a stone barn like piecing together a jigsaw puzzle.

On the other hand, farmers living in areas of rocky soil sometimes find themselves with piles of free building material just by clearing stones from their fields.

Left, top:

Pretty and practical

The ivy-covered stone walls of this Wisconsin horse barn are more than just unusually picturesque; they help hold heat in the winter and retain cool air in the summer—a definite advantage in the Midwest, with its seasons of extremes.

Left, center:

Wide-open space

The lack of hay doors suggests that the partial second story of this sprawling Kentucky octagonal barn is not used to store feed or crops for the calves housed below. Instead, its height allows heat to rise and escape through the second-story windows. These windows also allow plenty of natural light to flood the barn.

Below:

Shingle style

Shingle siding, round vents, and decorative carved corner accents make this Ohio barn from the early twentieth century look like a home or townhouse from the early twenty-first century.

Round Barns

The Shape of a Revolution

Right, top:

New fashion

Round barns came into fashion in the early to mid 1900s and were promoted as being a more efficient use of space than a rectangular barn—especially for housing dairy cows—since round barns were able to house more animals with less square footage of wall. Because less wall and foundation material is required to enclose the same square footage as a rectangular barn, round barns are less expensive to build, say round barn fans.

Right, center:

Efficient arrangement

This 1918 photograph shows how the stalls of a round barn were arranged like wedge-shaped pieces of a pie with the cows' heads toward the center and the "business ends" on the outside. Most traditional rectangular barns arranged stalls in two straight rows, with the cows' heads facing the outer walls and an aisle down the center between the rows.

Right, bottom:

Ahead of its time

The multi-leveled roof makes this fine round barn look like a spaceship out of an H. G. Wells novel. Are those lightning rods or antennae on the top?

This particular round barn is divided into stalls for thirty-seven horses. It could also hold 150 tons of hay.

Central silo design

In a 1911–12 report, the Kansas Board of Agriculture pointed out the benefit of having a round barn constructed around a central silo. This wood, brick, or concrete silo not only supports the roof but also "minimizes the labor involved in feeding the succulent silage to the dairy matrons."

Below:

However . . .

Round barns have their disadvantages, however. They are more difficult to build than the common rectangular barn, and the barn can't easily be made wider, longer, or taller as the farm grows. Extensions can be added, as on this dairy barn, but it is usually difficult to find a good place to connect such extensions to the main barn.

The style's popularity waned as farmers started storing hay in bales, which didn't fit as well as loose hay into round hay lofts. Many manufactured barn materials and equipment such as milking machines weren't designed for the curves of a round barn, and tractors, especially, were often too big to negotiate its corridors.

Barns as Billboards

Ads and Art along Country Roads

Treat your barn to the best

Arguably the most famous barn-side advertising campaign was done by West Virginia's Mail Pouch Tobacco. Barns bearing the company's name and slogan have dotted the rural scene since the early twentieth century. In exchange for permission to paint the Mail Pouch name on the side of their barns, the company gave farmers a choice of cash, tobacco, magazine subscriptions, or a fresh coat of paint for the whole barn.

Over time many of the old Mail Pouch barns have been torn down or painted over. Those signs that still can be seen are usually faded and worn. But their scarcity makes them popular with those who travel the back roads, and the signs have been protected by the federal government as national landmarks since 1965.

Pride

More common than even Mail Pouch barn signs are farmers' barn-side advertisements for their own businesses. And farmers go all-out, using more than just block letters and a simple slogan. This Illinois horse farmer used the barn's gable ends to commemorate the farm's prize-winning Percheron mare.

Above:

"Home of the Holsteins"

A hired professional painted the Holstein mural on the sliding doors of Zimmerman's round dairy barn. But thrifty, artistic farm folk often painted their own barn-side billboards.

Left:

Livestock exchange

There is no doubt what kinds of livestock this barn houses. In 1921, when this photograph was taken, horse-drawn carriages and wagons were still common and the average automobile went no faster than thirty miles per hour, which gave passersby ample time to read the fine print.

Teamwork and Timbers

Building Bigger and Better Barns

Right, bottom:
Coming together

Whether the barn was brand new or replacing an older barn, building it was a monumental event that brought the community together, as family, friends, and neighbors converged on the farm to help with the construction.

Sometimes a professional barn framer was paid to supervise the construction, but more often than not it was the farmers themselves who planned the design. Companies such as Sears, Roebuck or Montgomery Ward sold building plans for barns or sold the complete barn— plans, lumber, shingles, nails, and all—so all a farmer had to do was build it.

Right, top:
Raising the roof

Workers perch high atop timber scaffolding to nail down planks for the roof of a tall horse barn.

Right, center:
Mortice and pins

This early-1900s photograph shows the traditional mortice-and-pin method for constructing barns. Holes are drilled into the massive wooden main supports with a hand-crank drill. Then a wood chisel is used to shape the hole square. A square-shaped piece of wood is fitted into the square hole at a ninety-degree angle, and a wood pin is driven into the joint from the side to secure it. All of the timbers bear the rough-hewn cut marks of the rural saw mill.

Above:

Sky high

Barns are usually erected one of two ways. The first method is to frame the barn from the ground up, lifting piece by piece the posts, beams, and rafters to assemble the framework.

The second method is to fashion the main pieces of the framework—the bents—on the ground, then hoist each of them vertical and into position. The ground work requires only a few workers, but raising those huge pieces into place requires a huge crew. Half of the crew pulls the frame piece with ropes and pulleys, and the other half pushes it from behind with pikes.

Left:

Positioning shingles

With the roof boards and siding all in place, workers tackle the wide pile of shingles that need to be carefully positioned, one by one, overlapping like fish scales, in a layer over the entire roof. Luckily, the barn being constructed in this 1962 photograph is relatively small—only about 1,200 square feet—so there isn't quite as much roof to cover as on other barns.

A Home in the Country

The Classic Farmhouse

Right, top:

Elegant simplicity

For farmers of the early 1900s, creating a farmhouse with more architectural style and detailing than the average functional shelter required a generous amount of disposable income—especially since most farms have a good number of other buildings demanding repairs, updates, or expansions.

During the early twentieth century, most farmers sat squarely in the middle of the middle class, and their hard-working, middle-class values were reflected in the solid, local building materials, uncomplicated lines, and low-key ornamentation of their homes.

Right, bottom:

Custom L

Like barns, early American farmhouses were often designed to be versatile and easy to expand and upgrade as the family grew. The L-shaped farmhouse fit the bill nicely and was one of the most prevalent farmhouse designs of the Midwest. The kitchen is typically situated in one wing of the "L," with windows providing a cooling cross-breeze.

A typical midwestern farmhouse had two stories and was built of wood on a stone or brick foundation. Wide front porches were also a popular feature.

Left, top:

Cornbelt cube

This 1920s Indiana home was constructed in another familiar farmhouse shape—the "Cornbelt cube" or "four-square," many of which still line the streets of small towns and dot the rolling hills of the midwestern plains today. Four-square homes were typically built around a furnace, when such amenities as central heating arrived on the farm.

Left, center:

American original

The first settlers of the Midwest usually built log homes like this one, which dates from the late 1800s. As families went from subsistence farming to raising cash crops, they often left the solid-wall log homes for larger, better-insulated, wood-frame houses. Many kept their farms' original log houses intact, using them for storage or housing livestock, or as secondary living quarters.

Left, bottom:

Amenities

This 1922 Michigan home was quite remarkable for its time. Note the wires extending from behind the left wing and up from the right corner of the front porch. A high power line supplied this farm an electric current, and the house was equipped with such revolutionary appliances as an electric stove, electric iron, and electric washer. The majority of farms didn't feel the jolt of electrical power until the 1930s.

37

A Place for Everything

Other Farm Structures

Right, top:

Spring house

Springs bubble up from the ground in the hollows of rolling, hilly terrain, and in the early 1900s, spring houses were built over them to provide naturally cool, clean places to store milk or other farm perishables.

Unlike barns, spring houses and other farm outbuildings were usually long on function but short on style.

Right, center:

Ice house

If the spring house was the farm's refrigerator, then the ice house was its walk-in freezer. In the winter, blocks of ice were cut and hauled from nearby frozen lakes and ponds and stacked inside. With straw or sawdust between the layers for insulation, the large ice blocks would stay frozen well through the summer and into the autumn.

This 1917 ice house is made of concrete; most were wood or stone.

Right, bottom:

Milk house

Any dairy farmer will tell you there is a lot more to dairy farming than just milking cows. Cream needs to be separated from milk, the milk needs to be put in cans and kept cold, and the milk pails and other equipment need to be kept clean and sanitary. Such activities require a building unto themselves—a milk house, to be exact.

Barn without walls

A pile of loose hay takes up a lot more room than the same amount of hay compressed into a tight, square bale, which means that in the days before hay balers, farmers needed copious amounts of storage space for their loose hay. Once the hay loft had been filled, a farmer might use a hay shed, like this one in Iowa, to hold the remainder of the annual crop.

The fence around the bottom of the shed and a rope or two around the four corner poles hold the mound of hay in place.

Left, center:

Rest stop

Many an empty bucket, thirsty tongue, and dusty hand stopped by the pump on the path between the farmhouse and barn. Outdoor pumps were common on farms well into the 1950s, although they were not always so fancifully sheltered.

Below:

The essentials

Before the days of septic systems, field tile, and indoor plumbing, the privy was the place to go when nature called. Rain or shine, hot or cold, everyone's feet traveled the well-beaten path that led from the farmhouse to the outhouse.

CHAPTER 2

Mighty Machines

Left:

Burning rubber
An Allis-Chalmers WC pulls a steel-wheeled thresher down the road to its next job in 1934. The 1933 WC row-crop was the first tractor with rubber tires as standard equipment (steel wheels were optional). Mounted with Firestones, it cost $825.

Above:

Horseless carriages carrying horses
Sunday drives weren't the only thing a fancy automobile was good for. By modifying the hitch on the average livestock trailer, the family car could haul four-legged as well as two-legged family members.

Teamwork

Animals Power Early Implements

Right, top:

Partners in the field

Long before farmers took to the fields atop rumbling, rattling tractors, they looked across their fields from behind the steady rhythm and sway of animal haunches. Horses—as well as mules and oxen—were partners and companions in the field.

Right, center:

Long days, heavy loads

The transition from horses to total mechanical power was gradual, and animal power remained a mainstay on family farms well into the twentieth century. Many farmers first began using tractors for the heavy work of plowing and powering threshers but kept their horse teams for mowing, cultivating, and pulling wagons.

Given the variety of work that needed to be done, most farms had a minimum of two horses and many had upward of eight or ten.

Right, bottom:

Old faithful

A farmer rakes alfalfa with a one-horse dump rake in 1913. The motion of the fringes across the horse's back keep the flies from plaguing it.

Tractors made fieldwork faster and easier, but animals were more reliable and didn't break down like their mechanical counterparts. They didn't need replacement parts. They helped in the production of their own fuel, while at the same time providing fertilizer. And breeding the horses, oxen, or mules was a relatively easy way to increase pulling power.

Left, top:

Teamwork

Big and brawny, draft horses were bred to be true work horses. Teams were trained to work in tandem.

Plowing was hard work for both man and beast. The farmer pushed down on the single blade of the mold-board plow to keep it in the ground, while the animals dragged it through the tough, unbroken earth.

Full steam ahead

Robert Fulton's 1807 steamboat heralded a new era in American transportation. After conquering the waterways, steam crossed the country by railroad, and by the turn of the nineteenth century, it had powered its way onto the farm by breathing life into farm machinery.

This 1919 photograph shows a typical steam traction engine at work. The wooden water wagon provides the water to be heated into steam; the steam powers the traction engine; the traction engine powers the separator; the separator hulls the clover seed.

Heavy equipment

A massive hulk of steel and smoke, this coal oil–fueled steam traction engine was no mechanical mule—it was a mechanical dragon. Three men were needed to pilot the machine and its enormous fourteen-bottom plow across the fields in 1907.

The Dawn of a New Day

Steam and Kerosene Fuel the Farm

44

Left, top:

Avery kerosene tractor

A farmer proudly poses with his kerosene-powered Avery. His iron horse made this farmer somewhat of a pioneer, because in 1919, when this photograph was taken, tractors were still a novelty and hadn't made an appearance on the majority of farms.

At this time, tractors made for quick work—when they worked. Unfortunately, a broken-down tractor couldn't do any work at all. As early tractor manufacturers ironed out their iron horses' mechanical problems, many farmers stuck with their more reliable flesh-and-blood horse power.

Left, bottom:

Mogul kerosene tractor

Kerosene tractors, like this International Harvester Mogul, had to be warm in order to start. How do you warm a kerosene tractor? Build a little fire under the engine. Then just start 'er up and hit the fields.

Fordson and Ford

From the Roads to the Fields

Right, bottom:

Fordson Model F

Former farm boy Henry Ford made his mark on the tractor industry with his Fordson, the first tractor to truly threaten to take animals out of field work altogether. The Fordson's unusual (for the time) configuration of small, automotive-type steering gear up front with large drive wheels behind inspired curiosity; its low price—as low as $395 during World War I—inspired competition; and the prior success of Ford's Model T automobile inspired confidence. By 1923, just six years after the first one was introduced, the majority of gas tractors sold in North America were Fordsons.

Right, top:

Ford Model 9N

Although this photo was taken in 1941, the horizontal grille bars indicate this Ford 9N rolled off the assembly line in 1939, the first year of production.

The Ford 9N featured a three-point draft-control hitch designed by Irish inventor Harry Ferguson. Also known as the Ford-Feruson 9N, the tractor's four-cylinder engine included parts from Ford's successful V-8 automobile.

Right, center:

Ford Model 8N

Just as a decade brought changes to the way farmers hauled hay in from the fields, it also brought changes to Ford and its tractors.

In 1947, after breaking ties with Harry Ferguson, the Ford Motor Company introduced a new tractor model called the 8N. Ford then developed a complete line of implements to go with the red-and-gray 8N, thereby establishing itself as a full-line manufacturer.

Farmall

The First True All-Purpose Tractor

Left, top:

Farmall F-20

International Harvester was the first company to create a true general-purpose tractor—a machine that could do all of the farm's work, including row-crop cultivation. The new machine, appropriately called the "Farmall," made its debut in 1924.

The follow-up to the original Farmall Regular, the F-20, was one of IH's most popular tractors; about 150,000 F-20s were built between 1932 and 1939. This 1934 picture shows one of those F-20s with Firestone "groundgrip" tires preparing a seedbed.

Left, bottom:

Farmall Model M

In the late 1930s, International Harvester revamped its company logo, then smoothed away the square corners and rough edges of its Farmall tractors. One of the first of Farmall's new fleet of streamlined models was the M, the largest of four new models introduced in 1939. Note the rounded front grille.

Note, too, the farm service truck—no more having work stop to haul the tractor in for fuel or service. By bringing gas, oil, and the mechanic to the field, the truck helped farmers keep their tractors running smoothly with few delays.

John Deere

Big Green

Right:
John Deere Model D

With most companies producing four-cylinder tractors, John Deere chose to make its name with two-cylinder machines. These became known as Johnny Poppers or Poppin' Johnnies because of the engine's loud, distinctive popping noise, which could be heard across the fields.

Model D, the first tractor to bear the John Deere name, was the first generation of the yellow-and-green Johnny Popper family. The Model D enjoyed the longest production run of any tractor in farm history, from 1923 to 1953, during which time about 160,000 were made and shipped.

Below:
John Deere Model A

Introduced in 1934, the Model A was a row-crop tractor built to compete with International Harvester's Farmall. With its wide variety of configurations, the Model A and its less-expensive little sibling, the Model B, were Deere's most popular tractors. Both had long production runs and more than 320,000 of each were produced before production ceased in 1952.

Allis-Chalmers

Persian Orange Pride

Allis-Chalmers 20/35
Formed in 1901, the Allis-Chalmers Company was involved in steam power and electrical equipment, among other things. It introduced its first tractor, the Model 10/18 in 1914 and by 1926 established a separate division dedicated to tractor production.

Built from 1923 to 1930, the 20/35 was Allis-Chalmers's most famous tractor in the firm's early years.

Left, bottom:
Allis-Chalmers Model UC
The row-crop version of the Model U—the Model UC—had a power lift for a drive-in cultivator. The U and UC were the first tractors to appear in what would become A-C's trademark Persian orange color.

Minneapolis-Moline

A Prairie Gold Strike

Right, top:

Minneapolis-Moline Twin City Model KTA

The KTA was the second generation of general-purpose KT Kombination Tractors released by Minneapolis-Moline, the company formed in 1929 by the merger of the Moline Implement Company of Illinois, the Minneapolis Steel & Machinery Company, and the Minneapolis Threshing Machine Company. This 1936 wheat farmer is also using a Minneapolis-Moline Model A combine.

Right, bottom:

Minneapolis-Moline Model R

Toward the end of the Great Depression, hope for a brighter future was reflected in the brighter colors manufacturers began using for their tractors. Minneapolis-Moline's sunny Prairie Gold color debuted on its 1937 Model Z and continued to adorn its decedents, including the Model R.

This 1940s farmer did not take advantage of the Model R's most distinctive option—a fully enclosed cab. (Although Minneapolis-Moline's innovative enclosed cabs made headlines when they were introduced in 1938, they were expensive options, and enclosed tractor cabs wouldn't become popular on American farms until the 1960s.) However, he did choose a matching gold M-M #69 combine to go with his Model R.

Trendsetting Tractors

Introducing Farmers to the Future

Oliver Hart-Parr Row-Crop Model 70

With the Model 70, Oliver Hart-Parr told customers that this tractor needed 70-octane gasoline to run the tractor's quiet, smooth-running high-compression engine—making it the first tractor to run on high-octane gas. The Model 70 proved popular, and its success clearly proved there was a future for high-octane gas.

Massey-Harris General-Purpose (G-P)

Massey-Harris's General-Purpose was one of the first tractors—certainly the first widely available machine—to use four-wheel drive. It was engineered to keep all four of its equal-sized wheels on the ground even on the most rugged terrain. The G-P was criticized for a lack of maneuverability and engine power, however, and the model never sold well, despite improvements in subsequent models. Four-wheel-drive technology would have to wait about thirty years before hitting its stride and becoming commonplace on American farms.

Field Favorites

Some Famous—and Not-So-Famous—
Names from the Tractor World

Above:

Silver King R-66

Some of the 1930s' fastest tractors came from rail-road-locomotive builder Fate-Root-Heath and were named Silver King. The R-66 model was so named because of its 66-inch rear wheel spacing.

Right:

Case CC-3

Digging potatoes was just one use for the J. I. Case company's Model CC. As row-crop tractors gained popularity in the mid-1930s, Case brought out the CC and its sibling, the Model C, to compete with the Farmall and row-crop machines of other manu-facturers. One of the CC's distinctive features was its "chicken perch" or "fence cutter" steering arm.

Left, top:

Caterpillar Thirty

Since 1910 the name "Caterpillar" has been synonymous with the crawler, track-style movement. This movement was developed in the western United States, where regular tractor wheels got bogged down in the soft, wet soils. Like many of the early Cats, the Thirty was heavy, weighing nearly 10,000 pounds, but it was powerful enough to pull a five-bottom plow through a rye field.

Below:

Hart-Parr tractor

The Iowa-based Hart-Parr Company established the first factory in the United States to focus exclusively on gas traction engines. It is also credited with coining the term "tractor" to describe machines with such engines. Hart-Parr combined with the Oliver Farm Equipment Company in 1930, but this particular Hart-Parr tractor combined with an Avery.

Companies That Came and Went

*And the Distinctive Tractors
They Left Behind*

Below:

Indiana tractor

For every big, successful corporation like John Deere or International Harvester, there was a small company that didn't last in the competitive tractor industry. Many of these companies made only a handful of machines before their stars faded from the tractor universe.

The Indiana Silo & Tractor Company was such a company. It produced a single tractor—this lightweight, front-end-drive machine, reminiscent of a large garden tractor.

Right:

Avery motor cultivator

Known for its steam tractors, the Avery Company recognized that gasoline-powered machines were the wave of the future and developed a series of lightweight motor cultivators between 1916 and the early 1920s. Unfortunately for Avery, motor cultivators were a trend that passed quickly as the Farmall and other sturdy, general-purpose tractors hit the market.

Left, top:

Wallis Cub Jr.

The Wallis Tractor Company developed its tractors under the guidance of Henry M. Wallis, son-in-law of Jerome I. Case and president of J. I. Case Plow Works. The Cub Jr. was a smaller version of the Wallis Cub, which was one of the first tractors to have the transmission housing as part of the frame. The Cub Jr. was notable because all its drive components were fully enclosed.

Above:

Parrett tractor

Illinois's Parrett Tractor Company made tractors for only five years before it was purchased by Massey-Harris in 1918. Parrett built only a few models: the 10/20, the 12/25 Models E and H, and the 15/30 Model K.

Homemade Tractors

Ingenuity on Wheels

Right, top:
Lone ranger

Farmers who couldn't afford a brand-spanking-new Farmall or Fordson weren't left out of the mechanical revolution. Why buy new, expensive tractors when with a few spare parts from an old automobile, a blow torch, a little elbow grease, and a lot of ingenuity, farmers could build their own?

This 1923 farmer constructed his homemade cultivator from old car and truck parts as well as old horse-drawn implements. The machine's belts and wheels work like those on a separator.

Right, bottom:
Do-it-yourself Model T tractor

For the farmer who couldn't or didn't want to create a homemade tractor from scratch, there was help in the Sears Thrifty Farmer Unit, a do-it-yourself kit for converting the family car into a field tractor. "Don't let your old Ford or Chevrolet go to waste," exclaimed the Unit's ad in the 1939 Sears, Roebuck catalog. "Use it to make a practical general-purpose tractor that has the pulling power of from two to four horses, yet costs less than the price of one horse."

Tractor Tinkering

The Nuts and Bolts of Tractor Care

Gear work

A contentious farmer of the 1920s carefully works on the gear box of his John Deere Model D. If farmers who worked with animals had to be amateur veterinarians and grooms, the farmers who used tractors often became semi-profes-sional mechanics, getting to know all the gears, cyl-inders, nuts, and bolts in order to keep their me-chanical mules healthy.

Cleaning the air filter

Time spent fixing broken down tractors, or haul-ing them off the farm for someone else to fix, meant losing valuable time in the fields. So keeping on top of preven-tative maintenance—including regular oil changes and air filter cleanings—was worth a farmer's while.

Move 'em out

As the pictures of these pages prove, trucks were as important to farm life in the early 1900s as they are at the turn of the millennium. Trucks were especially useful to farmers who specialized in raising livestock or a specific crop, since such specialization meant they often had to transport big loads. The farm truck might also serve as the family car, depending on the family's finances.

In this 1926 picture, a hog farmer uses his Model T truck to haul a load of swine.

Right, center:

Diamond T

The bed of a large Diamond T truck is filled with newly threshed grain during the summer of 1934.

Below:

Pile it on

A pile of alfalfa rolls in from the field to the hayloft on the bed of an International truck in 1929.

Farm Trucks

Big or Small, They're All Made to Haul

Left, top:

Familiar fuel truck

The county farm bureau fuel truck was a familiar sight on many midwestern farms in the 1920s. Farm bureaus, or co-ops (short for "co-operatives"), supplied farmers with not only fuel but also fertilizer and feed. Some co-ops sent out trucks to pick up farmers' livestock and haul it to market.

Left, center:

Special delivery

Some farmers, like the Minnesota farmer who owned this truck, used their trucks to deliver the milk directly to the customers or, if their dairy operations comprised more than one farmstead, to transport milk and equipment between farms.

Left, bottom:

Full load

Milk trucks were standard on most dairy farms in the 1920s. Some were open-air models such as this one, others were closed-sided versions, such as the one shown opposite.

This particular truck was rigged up to carry almost two dozen cans, with room between the rows for carrying feed or other supplies.

Automobiles

Horseless Carriages Take on Farm Work

Facing page, bottom:

Versatile vehicles

No matter how fancy it was, the farm family's automobile, like anything else on the farm, had to pull its own weight. Most family cars did multiple duties, carrying everything from people to crops to livestock. When this photograph was taken in 1916, seat belts were not yet standard equipment, so farmers had to keep their calves "buckled in" with regular rope.

Right, top:

The multi-purpose Model T

Using interchangeable parts and mass-producing cars on an assembly line, Henry Ford made horseless carriages an affordable necessity for the average citizen, not just a luxury for the wealthy. In 1908, he introduced his famous Model T. Small, lightweight, and priced at a mere $850, more than 10,000 Model Ts were sold in its first year—an auto industry record at that time—and more than 15 million rolled off the assembly line before production ceased in 1927.

Model Ts sold to farmers often replaced work formerly done by wagons, work such as hauling wool to the cooperative shipping station.

Right, bottom:

Drive in

A crowded Iowa marketplace shows just how many farmers relied on their family automobiles to help with the farm work, as dozens of farmers line up to sell their loads of wool in 1919.

Beyond transport

With their hard-working four-cylinder engines, Model Ts were often the backbone of the farm. If they weren't used for transporting people, animals, or crops, the Tin Lizzies were also good for powering corn shellers, with a drive hub attached to the crank port. Model Ts also were often a handy source of parts for eclectic homemade tractors and other homemade machines.

Right, top:

Right of way

In the early days of automobile travel, horses and their loads had the right of way on country roads. Traffic laws in some areas, for example, specified that if a motorized vehicle approached a horse-drawn vehicle, the passengers of the former were to stop and throw a blanket over it to keep from spooking the horses as they passed.

Right, bottom:

Good old days

A farmer fills his trusty Hupmobile in 1934. Unfortunately, the days of the Hupmobile were numbered—the car was no longer made after the 1930s. The days of sixteen-cent-per-gallon gasoline also disappeared far too quickly.

On the Road

A Drive in the Country—the Way It Used to Be

Unscheduled pit stop
In the 1930s and 1940s, interstates were unheard of and most "high-ways" were made of gravel. Although the gravel of these roads was well maintained, for the most part, it made for some bumpy drives and took a toll on the cars.

Left:

Speed limits
Wooden signs such as this kept the speed demons of 1915 in check.

63

CHAPTER 3

Creatures Great and Small

Left:

Youngsters

A young farm lad prepares to feed his eager Holstein calf. Growing up with animals means farm children learn firsthand about the cycles of birth, life, and death.

Above:

Mule team

Many farmers will take mules over horses any day, citing the animal's stalwart strength, hearty physical build, and keen intelligence as reasons for their preference. Mule owners also praise their mule's loyalty, affection, and often colorful personalities.

Cattle Call

Livestock of the Bovine Ilk

Right, top:

Hereford cow and calf

A Hereford cow gently nuzzles her young calf during a sunny day in the pasture.

In the days of subsistence farming, cattle provided both milk and meat while also pulling farmers' plows and wagons. Eventually, horses and machines took over the labor, and as agriculture grew more specialized after World War II, farmers started maintaining larger herds of cattle and focusing exclusively on either beef or milk production.

Below:

Guernsey herd

An attractive herd of caramel-colored Guernseys makes its way from the barn to the pasture, ready to graze on rich spring grasses.

During the early 1900s, the typical commercial dairy herd consisted of twenty to thirty cows. After World War II, as milk machines began to replace hands and pails, the size of commercial herds increased—some having anywhere from fifty to a hundred cows. Today, dairy herds often have hundreds of cows.

Bossy goes to the fair

Proud parents take a picture of their daughter and her prize-winning bovine after a competition at a local fair.

Left:

Cow belles

A pretty Indiana belle poses with a pretty Jersey belle in 1927.

Tawny Jerseys and Guernseys are popular breeds of dairy cattle in North America, but black-and-white Holsteins are by far the most common. Other North American dairy breeds include the Ayrshire, Brown Swiss, Canadienne, Dutch Belted, Kerry, Milking Devon, Milking Shorthorn, and the Norwegian Red.

Milking Time

Tending the Matrons of the Dairy

Facing page:

Many hands make light work

A family of sisters puts their hands to the task in 1928. With a whole herd to milk by hand, anyone with strong enough arms and hands sat down to an udder to help the job get done quickly. Kids that didn't quite have the strength to milk were put to work hauling buckets to the cream separator, cleaning out stalls, feeding the animals, herding cows to and from pastures, or watching over grazing cows.

Left, top:

An exercise in humility

"I suppose milking cows by hand, and the attending duties, included much for teaching humility— one had literally to lower one's self below the cow's level to perform the task," writes farm boy, rural author, and cartoonist Bob Artley in A Book of Chores.

Left, bottom:

Tough work

Milking cows by hand required manual dexterity and forearm strength, especially if the cow was a "hard milker" and didn't let down her milk easily. Cows that had been out in the barnyard or pasture might come back to the barn up to their flanks in mud, which had to be thoroughly cleaned off before the pail was set down. You also had to beware the occasional hoof overturning a milk pail and the bristly tail brushing away flies. Finally, you had to endure the barn itself, with its wafting scents of manure and, in the summer, stifling heat and humidity.

Work Horses

Farmers' Four-Legged Field Hands

Right:

Four-hoof drive

Rural families generally used their horse team for all types of work, from hauling the family to town in a wagon to dragging a plow through unbroken soil.

Most farm horses can be considered draft horses—that is, horses trained to pull loads. Because most loads hauled on the farm were big and heavy, the horses pulling them were bred to be big and heavy. A typical draft horse can stand sixteen hands high and weigh a good 1,600 pounds or better.

Like the Belgian mares in this photograph, some draft horses are a particular breed, such as Belgians, Percherons, Clydesdales, Suffolks, or English. Most are blends of these popular thoroughbreds.

Below:

Dental check-up

Because horses were integral to the work of the farm, farmers often became equine experts with an ability to assess a horse's age and condition by the animal's stance, body form, gait, and overall condition. A quick examination of the horse's teeth tells the farmer how old the animal is.

Left:

Break time

You can lead a horse to water, and if he's been working in the field all morning, you won't have to make him drink. Horse teams can put in a long, hard day, as long as they have water breaks every few hours.

Below:

Fashion sense, horse sense

These draft horses aren't making a fashion statement—their floppy straw hats are purely practical. In the early 1900s, such hats were a common way for farmers to help their horses stay cool and keep the flies away from the animals' heads.

Right:

Mutual respect

Ol' Dobbin often was fondly re-garded as a family pet as well as a work horse.

Below:

Friends big and little

Despite their massive size and strength, many draft horses—such as this Belgian mare, pictured in 1915—were good-natured and gentle as lambs, carrying farm kids or other riders around on their backs as willingly as pulling a wagon full of corn. And what horse would snap at a youngster who comes to visit with a hatful of alfalfa?

Partners and Pets

Farm Horses Were Family Horses

The Pony Express

The Farms' Pint-Sized Steeds

Left, top:

Small tasks

No one was too small to work on the farm of the 1930s. A eight- or nine-year-old boy was plenty old enough to carry jugs of water to thirsty threshers waiting in the fields, and a pony broken to a harness was big enough to pull a one-seat cart.

Left, bottom:

Patient playmate

This pony is being remarkably patient while its playmates perfect their circus-style riding techniques.

Below:

All aboard

Because of their size, ponies couldn't heave heavy loads, tramp tirelessly over acres of field, or maneuver farm equipment as easily as draft horses could. But ponies are just the right size for giving young kids lessons in horsemanship, riding, and sharing with others.

Getting a trim

First a bath, then a pedicure. Two members of a "pig club" trim the foot of a Chester White in preparation for a competitive show in the 1920s.

Line up

A row of curious pigs forms along the fence to check out the passersby in 1913.

High on the Hog

The Farm's Mortgage Lifters

Left, top:

Good breeding

Hogs are well known for being fecund. Gilts are usually bred after the age of one year; sows can produce two litters a year with about six to twelve piglets per litter. At this reproduction rate, farmers can develop huge herds in a hurry, then maintain a healthy number of hogs and still have plenty to take to market. Because hogs are such a rapidly appreciating investment, farmers nicknamed them "mortgage lifters."

Left, center:

Changing shapes

From the early to mid-1900s, hogs were bred to carry lots of fat, mainly because lard had so many practical uses. After the 1960s, however, consumers abandoned lard in favor of vegetable oils and demanded meat lower in fat and cholesterol. Farmers responded by breeding and raising leaner hogs.

From Lambs to Rams

Sheep Raising

Right, top:
Wool supplier

A Rambouillet ram poses for a stately portrait in 1936.

In the days when farms supplied just about everything needed for daily life, sheep were essential livestock. Their fleece provided most of the fiber necessary for clothing, especially on northern American farms that didn't raise cotton. Since the development of synthetic fibers in the later twentieth century, the demand for wool has decreased, making sheep raising less profitable.

Right, bottom:
Quick clips

Shearing many sheep with hand clippers was physically exhausting, not to mention time consuming. This 1939 clipper was operated by a series of belts that ran down the hinged mechanical arms, like those of an old dentist's drill, and was mounted on the back of a truck. The man operating it most likely took his rig from farm to farm, shearing sheep for farmers. Such "freelance" sheep shearers often had a standard route, visiting the same farms spring after spring.

Left, top:

Watch your back!

The stereotypical ram will take any opportunity to make his presence felt, taking aim at anyone or anything. In truth, some rams, like this Shropshire, butt frequently and with little provocation, while others disregard even the most tempting targets. To be safe, it is best not to turn your back on any woolly head.

Left, bottom:

Loving care

A young boy becomes a surrogate parent to twin lambs, bottle-feeding them after their mother died. Rural kids frequently faced the reality of death while working with the farm's animals, but they also learned how to administer tender loving care.

77

Chicken challenges

Feeding and caring for smaller animals, such as chickens and other poultry, was farm work that the youngest members of the family could easily assume. But raising chickens was not without its challenges, because chickens are known for being easily frightened and not very bright.

Below:

Special delivery

One sure sign of early spring on the farm was flats full of chicks from the local hatchery arriving at the brooder house.

The Pleasures of Poultry

Of Chicks, Coops, and Clucks

Lunch counter

A farm wife feeds a flock of hand-some black-and-white, or barred, Plymouth Rocks in 1937. Barred Rocks lay highly desirable brown eggs (brown shells are thicker and stronger than white), and their meat was regarded as ideal for the broiler; these attributes, combined with the breed's striking appearance and reputation for being hardy and docile, made it one of the most popular breed of farm chickens prior to World War II.

Left, bottom:
Chicken dip

Although not the most pleasant way for a man or chicken to spend an afternoon, this 1930s farmer knows a quick lice dip will make his hens more comfortable in the long run.

White Gold

Eggs and the Hens That Lay Them

Right:
Help yourself
No conveyer belts or cages here. In the early 1900s, farmers rustled through the chickens' straw nests twice a day to pick out each egg and collect them in baskets.

Below:
Know your poultry
Like cattle, different chicken breeds are known for having different attributes; which breeds a farm raises depends on why they are being raised—for eggs, meat, or both. Leghorns, for instance, are known for laying white-shelled eggs and lots of them, making them one of the most popular breeds among egg producers.

Facing page:
Staples
Eggs were a staple at the farm table, and an average farm family could go through a dozen a week, if not more. So farms usually kept a healthy-sized flock of hens, and with a big enough flock, there might be some eggs left over to sell to the local farm co-op or grocery stores.

Farm Dogs

The Farmer's Best Friend

Above:

Buddies

Most farm dogs enjoy human companionship and relish being involved in farm work.

Right, top:

Helpful paws

Some canine breeds are well known for their abilities to herd livestock or perform other jobs. But most farm dogs are no particular purebred. They come in all shapes, sizes, and breeds, and even the smallest are often eager to help—or at least keep you company—when you're doing your farm chores, such as digging up potatoes.

Right, bottom:

Old faithful

Some farm dogs are trained for specific jobs. For instance, this dog was used to herd cows into the barn at milking time. Others might be used to round up or protect sheep or pigs.

The Rural Menagerie

A Variety of Farm Country Critters

Left, top:

Goat hitch

Some farmers keep goats on their farm for milk and cheese. Others maintain that having goats on pasture with horses will keep the horses from getting ill. Whatever the primary reason, the resourceful farm kid knows that goats are also handy for pulling a small cart or wagon load.

Left:

Flock of gobblers

Turkeys proved to be a profitable commodity for many farmers of the early to mid-1900s. However, because turkeys require a lot of special attention to keep them hearty and healthy, those farmers that kept flocks usually had a number of birds to sell on a regular basis, not just a few to sell occasionally, as often the case with chickens.

Left, bottom:

Farm felines

Nearly every farm supports a population of cats, which keeps the even larger population of field mice under control and out of the house and barn.

While mice are a problem, rats are bigger problems—literally. Larger, meaner, and more aggressive than mice, rats can take a toll on stored grain and be a health hazard to livestock. Luckily, cats usually kill off rats before the rodents grow large enough to do serious damage.

Left:

"No rubber ducky for me!"

Because of the space and variety of outdoor environments a farm affords, rural kids often are able to have pets—such as ducks—that just can't be easily accommodated in an urban setting.

83

The Lessons of 4-H

Promoting Agricultural Education

Right, top:

A little off the top

A young 4-H member uses a hand clippers to even out the wool behind his sheep's ears prior to a 1947 competition.

Almost every child who grew up on a farm after the 1930s participated in 4-H programs and clubs. These groups promoted agricultural education in rural areas by teaching practical skills, such as raising livestock, growing crops, sewing, cooking, and canning.

Right, bottom:

Center stage

Members strut their stuff in front of a packed coliseum during a 4-H club parade in 1950.

Making the grade

A judge inspects a row of dairy cows during a competition at a state fair. Many children form deep attachments to their "projects" after many months meticulously grooming, training, and caring for the animals. And many a child cries upon seeing their prize-winners sold after the final competition.

Left:

Poultry pride

A 4-H club member proudly poses with the three Buff Orpington chickens he raised in 1938.

CHAPTER 4

Farm Work through the Seasons

Left:

Warmth and growth
Summer brings warm days and endless blue skies, as row upon row of young, green crops flourish in both the fields and the family garden.

Above:

Autumn gold
Golden corn shocks and plump gourds mark the arrival of autumn on many American farmsteads.

The Rites of Spring

Plowing Prepares the Soil

Right, top:

Spring plowing

Springtime is just the beginning of the busy growing season. The earth, which has slept all winter under a blanket of snow, gradually begins to wake as the sun warms it. Farmers closely watch the calendar and the land to determine the ideal time to begin plowing—the first task in the months of fieldwork to come.

Right, bottom:

Turn over

A farmer plows under corn stalks and turns over the soil with a cultivator and rotary hoe in May 1932.

Facing page:

The good earth

In his autobiographical book The Land Remembers, *Wisconsin author Ben Logan lyrically describes the meeting of plow and soil: "The horses walked quietly. The loudest sound was the tearing of sod as the roots were cut or torn up and turned over. The sod talked. It said whether or not the roots were thick and healthy or weak and winter-killed. The soil underfoot talked, too. Good soil had a spring to it. Bad soil was hard and packed, with very little humus in it."*

When Seeds Meet the Earth

Planting Time

Right, top:

Corn planting

In the early 1930s, farmers drove horses from a seat on their planters. By the early 1950s, when this photograph was taken, the farmer's seat had moved off the planter and onto the tractor.

Right, bottom:

One at a time

As this 1930s farmer guides his team across the field, the plate-type planter he rides on drops seeds one by one into the soil in neat rows. The seed box near his right foot has an opening on top, beneath which a plate or disc rotates. The plate has holes in it, and as it turns, the seeds drop one at a time through the holes and down into a tube, which knifes the seeds into the ground.

The bin next to the farmer's knee holds fertilizer.

Walking the rows

After cutting a series of deep rows, a 1930s farmer drops in potato slips by hand. When he has finished, the rows will be covered by the horse-pulled drag parked in the background. The boy and dog add weight to the drag to make it more effective.

Below:

Family affair

The whole family pitched in to hoe rows and plant seeds in a farm garden of the 1940s.

91

Nurturing the Crops

Summer Fieldwork Stimulates Growth

Right, top:

Tilling corn fields

The Firestone tires of the tractor straddle rows of tender, young sweet corn plants as the machine digs into the soil between the rows in 1934. Loosening up the soil in this way helps it hold moisture. Cultivation also rips up weeds.

Right, bottom:

Contour cultivation

A 1940s farmer cultivates soybeans planted on a contour.

As the woman in this photograph can attest, farm and field work could be a remarkably egalitarian enterprise; there was so much work to be done that everyone pitched in to keep the farm running smoothly. In the early twentieth century, men, women, and children (many kids not even in their teens) all did their share of tractor driving.

Above:

Double fieldwork

After the mid-twentieth century, as tractors became more sophisticated, cultivation could be combined with spraying fertilizer or herbicide.

Left:

Bugs be gone

A 1919 potato farmer methodically makes his way through his field, scattering Paris Green insecticide over the plants with a brush in an effort to kill potato bugs.

93

Mowing

Hay Crops Fall to the Blade

Above:

Farm Jeep

This 1950s farmer pulled his mower with a Jeep instead of a tractor. After World War II, the manufacturers of Jeeps marketed their vehicles as farm equipment, adding power takeoff to the vehicles to run implements.

Left:

Ongoing mowing

Hay crops need to be mowed two or three times a year in most parts of the country.

While the Sun Shines

Putting Up Hay

Right, top:

Early baler

Picking up hay became easier and quicker with the development of mechanical balers. This early machine was a stationary baler made mobile by mounting it on the back of a truck.

Right, bottom:

Putting up hay

Pulling up just about a whole haystack at a time, farmers use a hay fork to transfer a load of hay from the horse-drawn wagon to the hay shed in 1918.

Facing page:

Hay days

In the days before balers, the whole crop was loaded in individual forkfuls onto an evergrowing pile on the hay wagon. Loading and hauling hay was tough, sweaty work, done in open fields with little shade to protect you from the high summer sun.

Bringing in the Sheaves

Harvesting Wheat

Hand work

A farmer sharpens the blade of his scythe in preparation for the August 1914 wheat harvest. Keeping the steel blade razor sharp was essential—swinging the scythe and cradle all day was back-breaking and time-consuming enough without having to deal with a dull-edged blade that would be unable to slice cleanly and easily through the wheat stalks.

Capping a shock

After grain was cut into sheaves, the sheaves were bound into bundles with twine, then the bundles were stacked, grain side up, into shocks or piles. Capping a shock meant laying an extra bundle across the top of the shock to protect it from the elements until it could be loaded onto a wagon and taken to the separator.

Above:

Mechanical binder

By the 1920s, binders were replacing the manual, scythe-and-cradle method of harvesting grain. The mechanical binder is an excellent example of how technology changed farm work. Compared with harvesting by hand, these binders cut more grain in a shorter amount of time, and they both cut and bound the grain—tasks that had to be done separately when performed by hand.

Left:

Driving a binder

The absence of reigns or whips indicates this farmer and his binder, photographed in 1936, are being pulled by a tractor instead of animals.

A welcome break

Threshing days began at sunrise and ended at sundown, and the work in between was hot and dusty. Members of the threshing crew labored hard to get the job done, and any chance to take a quick mid-afternoon break for water, coffee, sandwiches, and cookies was much appreciated.

Reaping What Has Been Sown

Days of Threshing Crews and Separators

Above:

Threshing scene

The growing cycle that began in the spring with sowing concluded in the late summer with threshing. This 1929 photograph captures nearly every aspect of the threshing operation—shocks standing in the far fields; a load of bundles coming in on a hayrack; workers atop another load pitching bundles into the separator; the separator depositing grain into a truck while blowing straw out into a pile; and a worker taking a well-deserved swig from the water jug.

Left:

Cooperation

The overall threshing operation comprised different jobs—from delivering loads to pitching bundles, manning the machine to stacking straw. Some of these jobs were more exhausting than others, and members of the crew often rotated, taking turns doing each job.

Pitching In
Many Hands Help with the Harvest

Facing:

Community Case separator

This Case separator was owned jointly by two farmers. Co-ownership of the massive separating machines was common in the 1930s; in some areas, a dozen or so farmers might own a single machine, and one farmer was usually the designated operator. The machine and its owners went from farmstead to farmstead, constantly working until each farmer's grain was separated and stored.

Left, top:

Prairie dinosaur

Former farm boy Jerry L. Twedt, in his book Growing Up in the 40s, *vividly and nostalgically describes the annual resurrection of the community separator: "... [A]ll attention was focused on the threshing machine as it prowled the countryside, devouring bundles of grain into its bowels. This prairie dinosaur frightened the horses, petrified small children, worried wives and mothers, and fascinated young boys, and, like the dinosaurs, is now extinct."*

Left, bottom:

Water boy

Before he was old enough to drive hayracks, pitch grain bundles, or stack straw as a full-fledged member of the crew, a young farmhand could learn his way around the separator while delivering jugs of cool water to grateful workers.

103

Both photos:

Technology strikes again

With a combine, a farmer could cut stalks and separate the grain immediately in a single pass through the field, skipping bundles and shocks altogether. Instead of having to wait their turn to use the community separator, then spending two to three weeks harvesting their grain, farmers could start their harvest whenever they and their fields were ready and do the job in a few days. However, without the yearly threshing to bring neighbors together, the sense of community in rural areas was diminished.

All in One

Combines Take Over the Harvest

Gradual changes

The owner of this Massey-Harris combine and Huber tractor helped pay for his investment by harvesting grain fields for fellow farmers, charging $2.50 an acre.

In the late 1920s, when this photograph was taken, the high price of combines prohibited many individual farmers from owning them. Separators and threshing crews were still the norm throughout most of North America. But combines gradually took over the grain harvest, and by the mid-1950s, community threshing machines and crews were a thing of the past.

Picking Corn

Harvest by Hand and Machine

Hand picking

Wide fields of crisp, golden corn stalks wait for the autumn harvest. Corn becomes dry enough to pick anywhere from late September to late November, depending on the part of the continent. Farmers could then take the early winter months to shell their corn and grind it into feed.

Although mechanical corn pickers were developed in the early 1920s, many farmers still cut down and picked corn by hand into the 1930s. They cut stalks using large, machete-like corn knives or, as here, with canvas gloves that had a sharp blade or steel hook fastened on the end.

Left, top:

Farmall two-row corn picker

Like binders and combines, mechanical corn pickers saved the farmer time and labor. Data from Purdue University (1929) says the average worker could hand pick only an acre or two of corn during a ten-hour day; a mechanical, single-row picker could take down about nine acres in the same amount of time.

Left, bottom:

Machines take the lead

A shortage of manual labor during World War I helped increase the demand for mechanical corn pickers. Although there was a dip in demand because of the 1930s Depression, after World War II, mechanical corn pickers like this one were in widespread use.

Right, top:

Gas-powered corn sheller

Early corn shelling machines were operated by hand cranks. But the arrival of small, gas-powered stationary engines made the once physically laborious process much easier. Even less-intensive tasks like chopping the tips and butts off seed corn, as these Ohio farmers are doing, was sped up by adding a gas engine to the homemade shelling machine.

Right, bottom:

Golden load

A waterfall of golden yellow kernels spills into the truck bed as fast as the workers can shovel ears onto the sheller's conveyor belt during the harvest of 1946.

Facing page:

Husking bee

In the days when corn was picked by hand, it also had to be husked by hand. With hundreds of bushels to husk, everyone—young or old, male or female—grabbed an ear and pulled.

Husking bees brought relatives and neighbors together, and thus turned into a social occasion, peppered with stories, songs, games, laughter, and perhaps even a little flirtatious chat. Whoever found an ear of corn colored dark red got to kiss the person of his or her choice.

Shucking, Shelling, and Shoveling

Readying the Corn for Storage

Autumn in the Orchard

Making Apple Cider and Butter

Above:

Autumn apple event

When apple orchards were a part of the family farm, making apple butter or cider was a familiar autumn event. Everyone pitched in to help pick, press, and pare the fruit, as well as watch the boiling pot and stoke the fire.

Right:

Press and pour

Dad squeezes the juice from fruit using the apple press, while Grandma pours the final product into storage barrels during the autumn of 1932.

Butchering Time

Stocking the Larder for Winter

Cold weather work

Hog butchering is best done in the late fall or early winter when the weather is cold enough to cool the meat quickly but not cold enough to freeze it.

Waste not, want not

No part of a butchered hog was wasted. Some parts, like the liver and pancreas, were cooked and eaten immediately, because they didn't keep. The head could be boiled for head cheese or its meat chopped up for mincemeat or sausage; the fat was cut into cubes and rendered into lard; the hams and loins were cured with salt and smoke; other meat trimmings were made into sausage.

Keeping Busy, Keeping Warm

Working in a Winter Wonderland

Digging out

Neither farmer nor tractor gets to rest in the winter. Although crop and field work are suspended, there are still plenty of farm chores that need to be done. And most farmers in Canada and the upper midwestern United States have to dig out from under heavy snowfalls. This northern Michigan farmer outfitted his Allis with snow chains and a blade to plow through drifts during the winter of 1954.

Winter pasture

Unless the temperature dips below zero, these Hereford cattle can usually spend their winter in the snow-covered pastures.

Left:

Cutting wood

Wood, corn cobs, and coal provided fuel to heat houses in the days before natural gas and electricity made it to the farm. Most families built up their wood piles well before the cold weather hit, but no one would pass up an opportunity to break out the cross-cut saw again and add to the pile if they found a downed tree.

Below:

Getting around

Today sleighs are romantic novelties and the stuff of holiday carols. In the early twentieth century, however, they were a practical mode of transportation and a fact of life on the farmstead where winter brought several feet of snow. Automobiles such as the Ford Model T were common on farms, but horses' hooves and sleigh rudders were more steady on snowy country roads than early narrow rubber tires.

CHAPTER 5

Domestic Living

Left:

Laundry made easy

Wringing laundry was just one household task that became easier when all-purpose, gasoline-powered stationary engines arrived on the farm.

Above:

Sweet corn

A young farm wife husks a few ears for her family's dinner before the rest of the bushels are shipped off to the town market.

Heart of the Farmstead

The Farmhouse Kitchen

Heart of the farmhouse

If the barn was the foundation of the farmstead, the farmhouse and its kitchen were the heart. Each day began with breakfast in the kitchen, and after various chores scattered them hither and yon, family members converged on the kitchen to wash up for dinner.

In the early to mid 1900s, farm wives were usually the keepers of the kitchen. From there, they presided over meal preparation, canning, laundry, and almost every other chore that kept the household—and its occupants—running smoothly.

Scrubbing up

All roads to the farmhouse passed through the kitchen. Here hands and faces were scrubbed, muddy boots scraped, and teeth brushed, as farm family members made the transition from hard work to well-earned rest.

It was unusual to see a sink with taps in 1915, when this photograph was taken. Instead, most farms had washstands—with a wash bowl, pitcher, and towel—standing near the door.

The 1920s ice box

An insulated ice box kept the day's perishable food chilled. The pan beneath it caught the water from the ice block melting inside.

Food from a Country Kitchen

Cooking, Baking, and Canning

Hot iron

Every surface of the mammoth cast-iron stove was hot to the touch, so this youngster wisely kept his hands to himself while watching his grandmother baste the roasting turkey. Although its fire constantly needed to be stoked with wood or corn cobs, a stove this size offered ample cooking room —more than enough space to cook all the food for a Sunday dinner.

Just like Grandma used to make

No frozen pie crusts, no canned filling, no Sara Lee. Wearing her trusty 4-H apron, a farm matron of the 1930s rolls out the crust for another homemade mincemeat pie. Preparing three meals for everyone working on the farm any given day meant many hours of hard work in the kitchen.

Both photos:

Canning day

Beans (left) and tomatoes (below) are just two of the myriad fruits and vegetables canned on the farm.

Sixty to one hundred years ago, it was common for North American farms to yield all the food the family needed for the entire year. Since the garden and fields lay dormant during the winter, preserving and storing a winter's worth of food was a matter of course.

As the produce of their gardens ripened throughout the year, most rural families canned jar after jar of beans, tomatoes, peas, corn, carrots, berries, plums, apples, peaches—just about anything and everything that could be grown in the garden throughout the spring and summer, plus meats from butchering done in late fall. Canning usually took the better part of a whole day, but it was well worth the effort to see glossy jars lining the cellar shelves and floors come winter.

From Udder to Butter

Separating and Churning

Right:

Separating

A milkmaid dumps a bucket of milk into an electric-powered cream separator of the 1920s. Separators such as these were the norm on big dairy farms, which had many gallons of milk to divide. When farms were smaller and had just a cow or two, the milk could be cooled in buckets or cans, then the cream skimmed off the top.

Below:

Churning butter

Buckets of smooth liquid cream are transformed into bowls of chunky butter in the churn. The churn in this 1928 snapshot was powered by an electric motor. After all the butter is scooped out of the churn, it was divided into smaller bowls to cool.

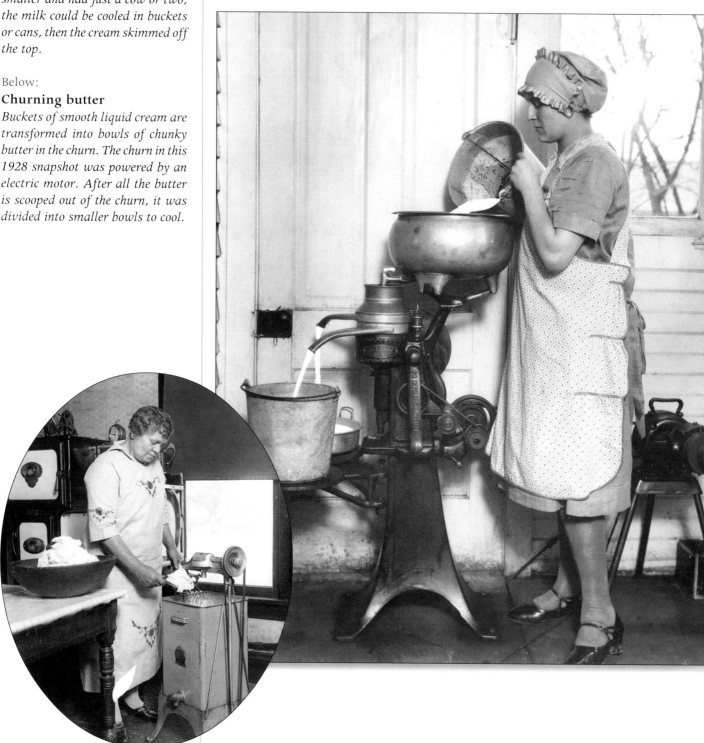

Hand Wash Only

Laundry in the Days of Washboards and Wringers

Wringing out

While many people fondly remember "the good old days," not too many yearn for the clothes-washing methods of those days. In her book All My Meadows, *rural author and farm wife Patricia Penton Leimbach describes the hand wringer as "a miserable miscreant propelled principally by profanity. . . . Nobody who hasn't grimly untangled a rag rug dragged back in by its tattered fringe, or unwound from the perimeters a twisted wad of undershirts, bra straps, socks, and apron strings, . . . then been ignominiously squirted in the eye by an overall pocket of dirty water from the final wash has the vaguest notion of the value of an unlimited water supply or the miracle of the automatic washer."*

Left, bottom:

Elbow grease

"Wash day" on the farm was an entire day devoted to the exhausting tasks of setting up the wash bench, scrubbing clothes by hand on a washboard, rinsing the clothes in tubs, squeezing them through a hand-cranked wringer, and hanging up the soggy items to dry outside or in the kitchen.

Right, top:

Pumping iron

In the days before indoor taps and faucets, any household chore requiring water began with a trip outside to the iron pump.

Right, bottom:

Drawing water

You can almost hear the creak of the wood as this young woman turns the crank on a timber windlass. Windlasses were less common than pumps for drawing up water from the well, but they could be found throughout the southern United States in the early 1900s.

Below:

Sausage making

Meat grinding and sausage making follow butchering as dawn follows night. There is usually a good pile of little meat bits leftover after the large hams, bacon, steaks, and roasts are dealt with, and these bits are perfect for grinding into burger or sausage.

All in a Day's Work

Sundry Household Chores

Left:

Steady hand

Wielding a hatchet with a steady hand was a practical and necessary skill on the farm, where the first step in preparing a fried-chicken dinner usually was stretching the bird's neck out on the chopping block.

Below:

Fill 'er up

Loading up the wood box just outside the door meant fewer trips to the main woodpile while cooking dinner.

123

Right, top:

Stitching britches

Spotting a ripped back pocket flapping on his behind, a quick-thinking, nimble-fingered mom snags her active toddler just long enough to stitch up his britches. Farm families' clothes are subjected to a lot of wear and tear, and there are always shirts in need of buttons, overalls in need of patches, and hems in need of mending.

Below:

Almost done

Most farm families' wardrobes were a combination of items bought from stores or catalogs and homemade clothes. Sewing circles gave women an opportunity to get together and exchange patterns, designs, and hints for making their own clothing.

Right, bottom:

Putting it together

A 1930s farm wife tunes in to the afternoon radio programs while running a seam through her new electric sewing machine. Before electricity arrived on the farm, women used treadle sewing machines powered by the motion of a foot pedal.

Keeping House

Making Sure the Outdoors Stayed There

Left, top:
Power

Some aspects of farm life have remained unchanged over the past hundred years—like dirt from the outdoors being tracked indoors by dusty work boots and the subsequent need for a powerful vacuum cleaner.

Left, bottom:
A good beating

Today, wall-to-wall carpeting is the norm in many American homes, and hardwood floors are a beautiful luxury. But fifty to a hundred years ago, hardwood was the most affordable, and thus the most prevalent, flooring. Instead of tacking carpeting to their floors, families covered them with carpets and rugs. Often made of wool, these coverings would be taken up and hauled outside twice a year to have the dust and dirt beat out of them.

Fruits and Labor

Working the Family Garden

Below:

Family work

For many farm families, grocery shopping required long trips down dirt roads to get to the nearest town and store. To save time and (more importantly) money, families raised much of their food on their own land. As this 1942 picture illustrates, children often helped tend the family garden, thus receiving an introduction to the miracles of soil and sun, while growing plants in the process.

Right:

New rows

A young farm woman plops bean seeds into a new garden row on a warm spring day in 1931.

Left:

Garden of green

On farms with ample land space, ever-important family gardens often became miniature fields in their own right.

Below:

Watch and learn

You're never too young to join Mom in the garden and learn the finer points of hoeing weeds. Babysitters and child-care centers were unheard of on farms of the early to mid 1900s; kids played or napped alongside working mothers, and when the children were large and old enough, they were put to work.

Tools of the Trade

Tinkering about the Workshop

Right:
A place for everything
Loaded with nuts, bolts, anvils, spare parts, and every imaginable tool—standard and homemade—the well-equipped farm workshop was ready to tackle any mechanical or carpentry challenge, from repairing broken tractors to sharpening dull implement blades to building kids' Christmas toys.

Below:
Handy man
A 1950s farmer breaks out the arc welder and dons a welder's mask to fix the hitch on his grain trailer.

Far right, top:
Forging on
The forge and anvil are standard equipment in most farm workshops.

Far right, center:
Repair work
A wobbly wheel brought this planter box into the workshop for adjustment.

Far right, bottom:
Sharp edge
A whetstone was essential for keeping a razor edge on sickle bars and other implement blades.

CHAPTER 6

Family, Fun, and Friendly Folks

Family values
Dinner was a chance for families to spend time together after long days of work and school.

Calling all farmers
The crank phone was the first type of telephone to arrive on the farm. Most rural telephones were party lines with a distinctive ring for each family along the line.

Radio Days
Connecting Farms with the World

Right, top:

Tuning in

Besides listening to the popular national soap operas, comedies, dramas, and news shows, farmers of the 1930s tuned into their local radio stations for daily reports on the weather and the livestock and grain markets.

Right, bottom:

Ear to the world

In rural areas where neighbors were often miles away, radio broadcasts offered a connection to a larger farming community and to the world.

Family time

Radios brought information and entertainment, and during the tense, trying times of the Great Depression and World War II, they brought encouragement and reassurance as well. In 1934, President Franklin D. Roosevelt used his "Fireside Chats" to introduce people to his New Deal programs; seven years later, newsmen, such as H. V. Kaltenborn and Edward R. Murrow, kept people abreast of changes in Europe.

Summer Fun

Long Days Leave Time for Play

Right:

The ol' swimming hole

When the weather was warm, it was tough for farm boys to keep their minds on chores.

Below:

Recreation

It might be hard for today's kids to imagine, but without television, computers, or video games, there were still plenty of ways to have fun. The farm gave kids acres of room to play sports and games, build tree houses, play with the animals, fish and hunt, or just wander around and explore nature. Children of the farm usually played as hard as they worked.

Above:

Ladies of the club

An outdoor bridge tournament brings the ladies of a rural neighborhood together on a breezy summer day in 1937. Church activities and local homemaking ("home ec") clubs were other opportunities for mothers and daughters of the farm to socialize.

Left:

Fishing trip

Some summer activities, like fishing trips with Grandpa, are timeless.

Back to School

Catching the Bus along a Country Road

Right, top:

Rural route

Georgia school kids ride to school in an open-air Ford Model T school truck in 1927.

Right, center:

All together

In the 1930s, children of all ages rode the bus together, because most schools taught all grade levels, from kindergarten through high school.

Right, bottom:

First day of school

Until the 1950s, when school consolidation became prevalent, most farm children lived within twenty miles or so of a country school. There were few hot lunch programs, so nearly every student carried a lunch pail.

Autumn

The Season of Leaves, Pumpkins, and Halloween

Right:
Fall break

Two 1940s farm boys stop for an after-school break by the creek before heading to the pasture to bring the cows in.

Below:
Halloween

Farms were usually too far apart for kids to go trick-or-treating, but that didn't stop them from carving jack-o-lanterns and creating other home-made decorations to celebrate Halloween at home.

Thanksgiving Dinner

The Feast That Brings Families Together

Special dinner guest
Almost every farm had a turkey or two running around, and if your farm didn't, one of the neighbors surely had a bird for you. Turkeys were often allowed to run loose in the farmyard or orchard, gobbling up whatever spilled grain or any other food they could find until November, when they were "invited" to Thanksgiving dinner.

138

Left:

Slow roast

Sliding the golden-roasted turkey from the oven and slicing it up on a platter are the last steps in the bustling feast preparations.

Below:

All together

Many sons and daughters established farmsteads of their own in the same rural area as their parents, so Thanksgiving could easily bring several generations together around the dinner table.

Winter Fun

Days of Skates, Sleds, Snowballs, and Snowmen

Right, top:

Ambush

Beware the young boys who lurk among the snow-covered evergreens, building up an arsenal of snowballs.

Right, bottom:

Skate date

The good thing about living in the country was that there was almost always a nearby pond, where court-ing couples could strap on their skates for a midwinter date.

Facing page:

Snowman

Mom puts the finishing touches on a robust snowman in 1936. Though there is still plenty of work to be done on the farm in winter, few can resist the allure of a farmyard of fresh snow.

Holiday Cheer

A Farm Country Christmas

Tinsel time

"No Christmas tree that ever came into the house was tall enough, short enough, full enough, shapely enough, or green enough to suit our kids," says rural writer Patricia Penton Leimbach in her book All My Meadows. *"Nor did we ever decorate a tree with our accumulation of trinkets—ancient and new, made or remade, elegant or rinky-dink—that we didn't appraise finally as splendid."*

Warm cookies

In many ways, Christmas on the farm is no different from Christmas in towns or cities. There are decorated trees, gifts of toys for the kids, and batches of warm sugar cookies. But in the country, especially in the early part of the twentieth century, Christmas trees could be cut from the woods behind the family's own house; toys were often crafted by hand in the farmer's workshop; and sugar cookies included lard from the hog butchered just a few months earlier.

Left:

"Santa's been here!"
Still clad in their footed pajamas, two 1940s farm boys happily discover the goodies that Santa Claus left by their fireplace.

Below:

Christmas morning
The joy of Christmas is in the giving.